50 Polish Ice Cream Recipes for Home

By: Kelly Johnson

Table of Contents

- Classic Vanilla Lody
- Traditional Polish Chocolate Lody
- Strawberry Lody with Fresh Berries
- Blueberry Lody with a Hint of Mint
- Raspberry Lody with Honey
- Lemon Lody with Zest
- Peach and Apricot Lody
- Wild Cherry Lody with Kirsch
- Apple and Cinnamon Lody
- Blackcurrant Lody with Cream
- Gooseberry Lody with Lime
- Rhubarb Lody with Vanilla
- Caramel Lody with Sea Salt
- Coffee Lody with Espresso
- Hazelnut Lody with Praline
- Almond Lody with Amaretto
- Poppy Seed Lody with Vanilla
- Pistachio Lody with Almonds
- Walnut Lody with Maple Syrup
- Chocolate and Orange Lody
- Chocolate and Chili Lody
- Dark Chocolate Lody with Raspberries
- White Chocolate Lody with Pistachios
- Milk Chocolate Lody with Hazelnuts
- Meringue Lody with Strawberry Swirl
- Honey and Ginger Lody
- Lavender and Honey Lody
- Rosewater Lody with Almonds
- Mint and Chocolate Chip Lody
- Lemon and Basil Lody
- Raspberry and Mint Lody
- Blueberry and Lavender Lody
- Plum and Cinnamon Lody
- Apple and Nutmeg Lody
- Sour Cherry and Almond Lody

- Pear and Ginger Lody
- Cranberry and Orange Lody
- Elderflower and Lemon Lody
- Apricot and Vanilla Lody
- Fig and Walnut Lody
- Melon and Mint Lody
- Peach and Rosewater Lody
- Kiwi and Lime Lody
- Mango and Passionfruit Lody
- Coconut and Pineapple Lody
- Banana and Peanut Butter Lody
- Peanut Butter and Chocolate Lody
- Caramel and Banana Lody
- Chocolate and Hazelnut Lody
- Chestnut and Vanilla Lody

Classic Vanilla Ice Cream

Ingredients:

- 2 cups heavy cream
- 1 cup whole milk
- 3/4 cup granulated sugar
- 1 tablespoon pure vanilla extract
- 1 vanilla bean (optional, for extra flavor)
- Pinch of salt

Instructions:

1. **Combine the base ingredients**: In a mixing bowl, whisk together the heavy cream, whole milk, sugar, and a pinch of salt until the sugar is fully dissolved.
2. **Vanilla bean (optional)**: If using a vanilla bean, slice it open and scrape the seeds into the mixture. Add the pod to the bowl as well. Heat the mixture over medium heat in a saucepan until it is just about to simmer, but do not let it boil. Remove from heat, cover, and let it infuse for about 15 minutes. Afterward, discard the vanilla pod.
3. **Chill the mixture**: Let the mixture cool to room temperature, then transfer it to the refrigerator and chill for at least 2 hours or until it's thoroughly cold.
4. **Churn the ice cream**: Pour the chilled mixture into an ice cream maker and churn according to the manufacturer's instructions, typically for about 20-25 minutes, until the ice cream reaches a soft-serve consistency.
5. **Freeze to firm up**: Transfer the ice cream to an airtight container and freeze for at least 4 hours or overnight to firm up.
6. **Serve**: Once ready, scoop and serve this creamy, classic vanilla treat!

Traditional Polish Chocolate Lody

Ingredients:

- 2 cups heavy cream
- 1 cup whole milk
- 3/4 cup granulated sugar
- 1/2 cup unsweetened cocoa powder
- 1/2 cup dark chocolate (chopped)
- 1 tablespoon vanilla extract
- Pinch of salt

Instructions:

1. In a saucepan, combine the cocoa powder, sugar, and salt. Add the milk and heat over medium heat, stirring constantly, until the mixture is warm and the cocoa powder has dissolved.
2. Add the chopped dark chocolate and stir until melted and smooth.
3. Remove from heat and let the mixture cool to room temperature.
4. In a bowl, whisk together the heavy cream and vanilla extract.
5. Pour the cooled chocolate mixture into the cream and mix well.
6. Churn the mixture in an ice cream maker according to the manufacturer's instructions.
7. Freeze for 4-6 hours to firm up before serving.

Strawberry Lody with Fresh Berries

Ingredients:

- 2 cups fresh strawberries (hulled and halved)
- 1 cup heavy cream
- 1 cup whole milk
- 3/4 cup granulated sugar
- 1 tablespoon lemon juice
- 1 teaspoon vanilla extract

Instructions:

1. In a blender or food processor, combine the strawberries, sugar, and lemon juice. Blend until smooth.
2. Pour the strawberry mixture into a mixing bowl, then add the cream, milk, and vanilla extract.
3. Stir the mixture until everything is well combined.
4. Churn the mixture in an ice cream maker according to the manufacturer's instructions.
5. During the last few minutes of churning, add fresh whole strawberries to the mixture for extra texture and flavor.
6. Freeze for 4-6 hours before serving.

Blueberry Lody with a Hint of Mint

Ingredients:

- 2 cups fresh blueberries
- 1 cup heavy cream
- 1 cup whole milk
- 3/4 cup granulated sugar
- 1 tablespoon fresh mint (chopped)
- 1 teaspoon lemon juice

Instructions:

1. In a blender, combine the blueberries, sugar, and lemon juice. Blend until smooth.
2. Add the chopped mint and pulse gently to incorporate.
3. In a bowl, combine the blueberry-mint mixture with the heavy cream and milk.
4. Stir until well combined.
5. Churn the mixture in an ice cream maker according to the manufacturer's instructions.
6. Freeze for 4-6 hours to firm up before serving.

Raspberry Lody with Honey

Ingredients:

- 2 cups fresh raspberries
- 1 cup heavy cream
- 1 cup whole milk
- 1/2 cup honey
- 1 teaspoon vanilla extract

Instructions:

1. In a blender or food processor, combine the raspberries and honey. Blend until smooth.
2. Pour the raspberry mixture into a bowl and stir in the heavy cream, milk, and vanilla extract.
3. Mix until well combined.
4. Churn the mixture in an ice cream maker according to the manufacturer's instructions.
5. Freeze for 4-6 hours to firm up before serving.

Lemon Lody with Zest

Ingredients:

- 2 cups heavy cream
- 1 cup whole milk
- 3/4 cup granulated sugar
- Zest of 2 lemons
- 1/4 cup fresh lemon juice
- 1 teaspoon vanilla extract

Instructions:

1. In a mixing bowl, whisk together the cream, milk, sugar, and vanilla extract.
2. Add the lemon zest and lemon juice to the mixture and stir well.
3. Pour the mixture into an ice cream maker and churn according to the manufacturer's instructions.
4. Freeze for 4-6 hours until firm.

Peach and Apricot Lody

Ingredients:

- 2 cups fresh peaches (pitted and chopped)
- 1 cup fresh apricots (pitted and chopped)
- 1 cup heavy cream
- 1 cup whole milk
- 3/4 cup granulated sugar
- 1 tablespoon lemon juice

Instructions:

1. In a blender, combine the peaches, apricots, sugar, and lemon juice. Blend until smooth.
2. Add the heavy cream and milk to the mixture and stir until combined.
3. Churn the mixture in an ice cream maker according to the manufacturer's instructions.
4. Freeze for 4-6 hours to firm up before serving.

Wild Cherry Lody with Kirsch

Ingredients:

- 2 cups fresh wild cherries (pitted)
- 1/2 cup granulated sugar
- 1 tablespoon Kirsch (cherry brandy)
- 1 cup heavy cream
- 1 cup whole milk
- 1 teaspoon vanilla extract

Instructions:

1. In a saucepan, cook the cherries with sugar over medium heat until softened and syrupy, about 10 minutes.
2. Stir in the Kirsch and remove from heat to cool.
3. Once cooled, blend the mixture until smooth.
4. Combine the cherry mixture with the heavy cream, milk, and vanilla extract. Stir to combine.
5. Churn in an ice cream maker according to the manufacturer's instructions.
6. Freeze for 4-6 hours before serving.

Apple and Cinnamon Lody

Ingredients:

- 2 cups apples (peeled and chopped)
- 1/2 cup granulated sugar
- 1/2 teaspoon ground cinnamon
- 1 cup heavy cream
- 1 cup whole milk
- 1 teaspoon vanilla extract

Instructions:

1. In a saucepan, cook the apples with sugar and cinnamon over medium heat until soft, about 10 minutes.
2. Blend the apple mixture until smooth and let it cool.
3. Combine the apple puree with the heavy cream, milk, and vanilla extract.
4. Stir until well combined.
5. Churn the mixture in an ice cream maker according to the manufacturer's instructions.
6. Freeze for 4-6 hours to firm up.

Blackcurrant Lody with Cream

Ingredients:

- 2 cups fresh blackcurrants (or frozen)
- 3/4 cup granulated sugar
- 1 cup heavy cream
- 1 cup whole milk
- 1 teaspoon vanilla extract

Instructions:

1. In a blender, combine the blackcurrants and sugar. Blend until smooth.
2. Add the heavy cream, milk, and vanilla extract, and mix well.
3. Churn the mixture in an ice cream maker according to the manufacturer's instructions.
4. Freeze for 4-6 hours to firm up before serving.

Gooseberry Lody with Lime

Ingredients:

- 2 cups fresh gooseberries (or frozen)
- 1/2 cup granulated sugar
- Zest of 1 lime
- 1 tablespoon lime juice
- 1 cup heavy cream
- 1 cup whole milk

Instructions:

1. In a saucepan, cook the gooseberries and sugar over medium heat until softened, about 10 minutes.
2. Blend the mixture until smooth, then stir in the lime zest and lime juice.
3. Add the heavy cream and milk, and mix well.
4. Churn in an ice cream maker according to the manufacturer's instructions.
5. Freeze for 4-6 hours until firm.

Rhubarb Lody with Vanilla

Ingredients:

- 2 cups fresh rhubarb (chopped)
- 1/2 cup granulated sugar
- 1 teaspoon vanilla extract
- 1 cup heavy cream
- 1 cup whole milk

Instructions:

1. In a saucepan, cook the rhubarb with sugar over medium heat until tender, about 10 minutes.
2. Blend the rhubarb mixture until smooth.
3. Stir in the vanilla extract, heavy cream, and milk.
4. Mix well and churn in an ice cream maker according to the manufacturer's instructions.
5. Freeze for 4-6 hours to firm up before serving.

Caramel Lody with Sea Salt

Ingredients:

- 1 cup heavy cream
- 1 cup whole milk
- 3/4 cup granulated sugar
- 1/4 cup brown sugar
- 1 teaspoon vanilla extract
- 1/2 teaspoon sea salt

Instructions:

1. In a saucepan, melt the sugar and brown sugar over medium heat until caramelized, about 5-7 minutes.
2. Slowly whisk in the heavy cream and milk until smooth.
3. Add the vanilla extract and sea salt, then stir to combine.
4. Let the caramel mixture cool to room temperature, then churn in an ice cream maker.
5. Freeze for 4-6 hours until firm.

Coffee Lody with Espresso

Ingredients:

- 2 cups heavy cream
- 1 cup whole milk
- 1/2 cup granulated sugar
- 2 shots of espresso (cooled)
- 1 teaspoon vanilla extract

Instructions:

1. In a bowl, whisk together the heavy cream, milk, sugar, and vanilla extract.
2. Stir in the cooled espresso and mix until fully combined.
3. Churn the mixture in an ice cream maker according to the manufacturer's instructions.
4. Freeze for 4-6 hours before serving.

Hazelnut Lody with Praline

Ingredients:

- 2 cups heavy cream
- 1 cup whole milk
- 3/4 cup granulated sugar
- 1/2 cup hazelnut paste or hazelnut butter
- 1/2 cup praline (crushed)
- 1 teaspoon vanilla extract

Instructions:

1. In a mixing bowl, whisk together the heavy cream, milk, sugar, and vanilla extract until the sugar is dissolved.
2. Stir in the hazelnut paste or hazelnut butter and mix until smooth.
3. Add the crushed praline and mix well.
4. Churn the mixture in an ice cream maker according to the manufacturer's instructions.
5. Freeze for 4-6 hours to firm up.

Almond Lody with Amaretto

Ingredients:

- 2 cups heavy cream
- 1 cup whole milk
- 3/4 cup granulated sugar
- 1/2 cup almond paste
- 2 tablespoons Amaretto liqueur
- 1 teaspoon vanilla extract

Instructions:

1. In a mixing bowl, whisk together the heavy cream, milk, sugar, and vanilla extract until the sugar is dissolved.
2. Add the almond paste and Amaretto, mixing until smooth.
3. Churn the mixture in an ice cream maker according to the manufacturer's instructions.
4. Freeze for 4-6 hours to firm up.

Poppy Seed Lody with Vanilla

Ingredients:

- 2 cups heavy cream
- 1 cup whole milk
- 3/4 cup granulated sugar
- 2 tablespoons poppy seeds
- 1 teaspoon vanilla extract

Instructions:

1. In a saucepan, heat the cream and milk over medium heat until warm.
2. Stir in the sugar and poppy seeds, then remove from heat.
3. Add the vanilla extract and let the mixture cool.
4. Pour into an ice cream maker and churn according to the manufacturer's instructions.
5. Freeze for 4-6 hours until firm.

Pistachio Lody with Almonds

Ingredients:

- 2 cups heavy cream
- 1 cup whole milk
- 3/4 cup granulated sugar
- 1/2 cup pistachio paste
- 1/4 cup chopped almonds
- 1 teaspoon vanilla extract

Instructions:

1. In a bowl, combine the heavy cream, milk, sugar, and vanilla extract. Whisk until smooth.
2. Stir in the pistachio paste and mix well.
3. Churn the mixture in an ice cream maker according to the manufacturer's instructions.
4. During the last few minutes of churning, add the chopped almonds for extra texture.
5. Freeze for 4-6 hours until firm.

Walnut Lody with Maple Syrup

Ingredients:

- 2 cups heavy cream
- 1 cup whole milk
- 3/4 cup granulated sugar
- 1/4 cup maple syrup
- 1/2 cup chopped walnuts
- 1 teaspoon vanilla extract

Instructions:

1. In a mixing bowl, whisk together the heavy cream, milk, sugar, vanilla extract, and maple syrup.
2. Stir in the chopped walnuts.
3. Churn the mixture in an ice cream maker according to the manufacturer's instructions.
4. Freeze for 4-6 hours until firm.

Chocolate and Orange Lody

Ingredients:

- 2 cups heavy cream
- 1 cup whole milk
- 3/4 cup granulated sugar
- 1/2 cup dark chocolate (chopped)
- Zest of 1 orange
- 1 teaspoon orange juice
- 1 teaspoon vanilla extract

Instructions:

1. Melt the dark chocolate over low heat, then let it cool slightly.
2. In a mixing bowl, combine the heavy cream, milk, sugar, vanilla extract, and orange juice. Whisk until smooth.
3. Stir in the melted chocolate and orange zest.
4. Churn the mixture in an ice cream maker according to the manufacturer's instructions.
5. Freeze for 4-6 hours to firm up.

Chocolate and Chili Lody

Ingredients:

- 2 cups heavy cream
- 1 cup whole milk
- 3/4 cup granulated sugar
- 1/2 cup dark chocolate (chopped)
- 1/2 teaspoon chili powder
- 1 teaspoon vanilla extract

Instructions:

1. Melt the dark chocolate over low heat, then let it cool slightly.
2. In a mixing bowl, whisk together the cream, milk, sugar, and vanilla extract.
3. Stir in the melted chocolate and chili powder until well combined.
4. Churn the mixture in an ice cream maker according to the manufacturer's instructions.
5. Freeze for 4-6 hours to firm up.

Dark Chocolate Lody with Raspberries

Ingredients:

- 2 cups heavy cream
- 1 cup whole milk
- 3/4 cup granulated sugar
- 1/2 cup dark chocolate (chopped)
- 1 cup fresh raspberries
- 1 teaspoon vanilla extract

Instructions:

1. Melt the dark chocolate over low heat, then let it cool slightly.
2. In a mixing bowl, whisk together the heavy cream, milk, sugar, and vanilla extract.
3. Stir in the melted chocolate and combine well.
4. Gently fold in the raspberries.
5. Churn in an ice cream maker according to the manufacturer's instructions.
6. Freeze for 4-6 hours to firm up.

White Chocolate Lody with Pistachios

Ingredients:

- 2 cups heavy cream
- 1 cup whole milk
- 3/4 cup granulated sugar
- 1/2 cup white chocolate (chopped)
- 1/4 cup pistachios (chopped)
- 1 teaspoon vanilla extract

Instructions:

1. Melt the white chocolate over low heat, then let it cool slightly.
2. In a mixing bowl, whisk together the cream, milk, sugar, and vanilla extract.
3. Stir in the melted white chocolate and mix until smooth.
4. Churn the mixture in an ice cream maker according to the manufacturer's instructions.
5. Add the chopped pistachios during the last few minutes of churning.
6. Freeze for 4-6 hours until firm.

Milk Chocolate Lody with Hazelnuts

Ingredients:

- 2 cups heavy cream
- 1 cup whole milk
- 3/4 cup granulated sugar
- 1/2 cup milk chocolate (chopped)
- 1/2 cup hazelnuts (toasted and chopped)
- 1 teaspoon vanilla extract

Instructions:

1. In a saucepan, heat the heavy cream and milk over medium heat until warm.
2. Add the sugar and stir until dissolved.
3. Melt the milk chocolate and stir it into the cream mixture.
4. Remove from heat and let the mixture cool slightly before adding the vanilla extract.
5. Churn the mixture in an ice cream maker according to the manufacturer's instructions.
6. Fold in the toasted and chopped hazelnuts during the last few minutes of churning.
7. Freeze for 4-6 hours to firm up.

Meringue Lody with Strawberry Swirl

Ingredients:

- 2 cups heavy cream
- 1 cup whole milk
- 3/4 cup granulated sugar
- 1 teaspoon vanilla extract
- 1/2 cup meringue (crushed)
- 1/2 cup fresh strawberries (pureed)

Instructions:

1. In a mixing bowl, whisk together the heavy cream, milk, sugar, and vanilla extract until smooth.
2. Puree the strawberries and swirl them into the cream mixture.
3. Churn the mixture in an ice cream maker according to the manufacturer's instructions.
4. Gently fold in the crushed meringue at the end of churning.
5. Freeze for 4-6 hours until firm.

Honey and Ginger Lody

Ingredients:

- 2 cups heavy cream
- 1 cup whole milk
- 3/4 cup honey
- 1/2 teaspoon ground ginger
- 1 teaspoon vanilla extract

Instructions:

1. In a saucepan, heat the heavy cream and milk until warm.
2. Stir in the honey and ground ginger, and whisk until fully combined.
3. Let the mixture cool to room temperature, then add the vanilla extract.
4. Churn the mixture in an ice cream maker according to the manufacturer's instructions.
5. Freeze for 4-6 hours to firm up.

Lavender and Honey Lody

Ingredients:

- 2 cups heavy cream
- 1 cup whole milk
- 3/4 cup honey
- 1 tablespoon dried lavender flowers
- 1 teaspoon vanilla extract

Instructions:

1. In a saucepan, combine the heavy cream and milk. Heat over medium heat until warm.
2. Stir in the honey and dried lavender flowers. Let steep for 10-15 minutes.
3. Strain out the lavender and let the mixture cool to room temperature.
4. Add the vanilla extract and churn the mixture in an ice cream maker according to the manufacturer's instructions.
5. Freeze for 4-6 hours until firm.

Rosewater Lody with Almonds

Ingredients:

- 2 cups heavy cream
- 1 cup whole milk
- 3/4 cup granulated sugar
- 1 teaspoon rosewater
- 1/2 cup chopped almonds (toasted)

Instructions:

1. In a mixing bowl, whisk together the heavy cream, milk, sugar, and rosewater until smooth.
2. Churn the mixture in an ice cream maker according to the manufacturer's instructions.
3. During the last few minutes of churning, add the toasted chopped almonds.
4. Freeze for 4-6 hours to firm up.

Mint and Chocolate Chip Lody

Ingredients:

- 2 cups heavy cream
- 1 cup whole milk
- 3/4 cup granulated sugar
- 1 teaspoon peppermint extract
- 1/2 cup dark chocolate chips

Instructions:

1. In a mixing bowl, whisk together the heavy cream, milk, sugar, and peppermint extract until smooth.
2. Churn the mixture in an ice cream maker according to the manufacturer's instructions.
3. During the last few minutes of churning, add the dark chocolate chips.
4. Freeze for 4-6 hours until firm.

Lemon and Basil Lody

Ingredients:

- 2 cups heavy cream
- 1 cup whole milk
- 3/4 cup granulated sugar
- Zest of 1 lemon
- 2 tablespoons fresh basil (chopped)
- 1 teaspoon lemon juice

Instructions:

1. In a saucepan, heat the heavy cream and milk over medium heat.
2. Add the sugar and lemon zest, and stir until the sugar is dissolved.
3. Remove from heat and stir in the fresh basil and lemon juice.
4. Let the mixture cool to room temperature before churning in an ice cream maker according to the manufacturer's instructions.
5. Freeze for 4-6 hours to firm up.

Raspberry and Mint Lody

Ingredients:

- 2 cups heavy cream
- 1 cup whole milk
- 3/4 cup granulated sugar
- 1 cup fresh raspberries
- 1 teaspoon mint extract

Instructions:

1. In a mixing bowl, whisk together the heavy cream, milk, and sugar until smooth.
2. Puree the raspberries and mix into the cream mixture.
3. Add the mint extract and stir well.
4. Churn the mixture in an ice cream maker according to the manufacturer's instructions.
5. Freeze for 4-6 hours until firm.

Blueberry and Lavender Lody

Ingredients:

- 2 cups heavy cream
- 1 cup whole milk
- 3/4 cup granulated sugar
- 1 cup fresh blueberries
- 1 tablespoon dried lavender flowers

Instructions:

1. In a saucepan, heat the heavy cream and milk over medium heat.
2. Add the sugar and lavender flowers. Stir until the sugar dissolves and the mixture is warm.
3. Let steep for 10-15 minutes, then strain out the lavender.
4. Puree the blueberries and stir into the cream mixture.
5. Churn the mixture in an ice cream maker according to the manufacturer's instructions.
6. Freeze for 4-6 hours to firm up.

Plum and Cinnamon Lody

Ingredients:

- 2 cups heavy cream
- 1 cup whole milk
- 3/4 cup granulated sugar
- 1 teaspoon ground cinnamon
- 1 cup fresh plums (pitted and chopped)
- 1 teaspoon vanilla extract

Instructions:

1. In a saucepan, heat the heavy cream and milk over medium heat.
2. Add the sugar and ground cinnamon, stirring until dissolved.
3. Once the mixture is warm, add the chopped plums and cook for 5-10 minutes to soften.
4. Remove from heat and let it cool before blending the plum mixture into a smooth puree.
5. Stir in the vanilla extract and churn the mixture in an ice cream maker according to the manufacturer's instructions.
6. Freeze for 4-6 hours until firm.

Apple and Nutmeg Lody

Ingredients:

- 2 cups heavy cream
- 1 cup whole milk
- 3/4 cup granulated sugar
- 1/2 teaspoon ground nutmeg
- 2 apples (peeled, cored, and chopped)
- 1 teaspoon vanilla extract

Instructions:

1. In a saucepan, heat the heavy cream and milk over medium heat.
2. Add the sugar and ground nutmeg, stirring until dissolved.
3. Cook the chopped apples until soft, about 10 minutes.
4. Blend the apples into a smooth puree and mix with the cream mixture.
5. Stir in the vanilla extract and churn in an ice cream maker.
6. Freeze for 4-6 hours to firm up.

Sour Cherry and Almond Lody

Ingredients:

- 2 cups heavy cream
- 1 cup whole milk
- 3/4 cup granulated sugar
- 1 cup sour cherries (pitted)
- 1/2 teaspoon almond extract
- 1/2 cup chopped almonds (toasted)

Instructions:

1. In a saucepan, heat the heavy cream and milk over medium heat.
2. Add the sugar and stir until dissolved.
3. Puree the sour cherries and mix into the cream mixture.
4. Add the almond extract and stir well.
5. Churn the mixture in an ice cream maker.
6. During the last few minutes of churning, add the toasted chopped almonds.
7. Freeze for 4-6 hours to firm up.

Pear and Ginger Lody

Ingredients:

- 2 cups heavy cream
- 1 cup whole milk
- 3/4 cup granulated sugar
- 2 pears (peeled and chopped)
- 1 tablespoon grated fresh ginger
- 1 teaspoon vanilla extract

Instructions:

1. In a saucepan, heat the heavy cream and milk over medium heat.
2. Add the sugar and stir until dissolved.
3. Cook the pears and ginger together until soft, about 10 minutes.
4. Blend the pear and ginger mixture into a smooth puree and add to the cream mixture.
5. Stir in the vanilla extract and churn in an ice cream maker.
6. Freeze for 4-6 hours to firm up.

Cranberry and Orange Lody

Ingredients:

- 2 cups heavy cream
- 1 cup whole milk
- 3/4 cup granulated sugar
- 1 cup fresh cranberries
- Zest and juice of 1 orange
- 1 teaspoon vanilla extract

Instructions:

1. In a saucepan, heat the cranberries, heavy cream, and milk over medium heat until the cranberries begin to burst.
2. Add the sugar and stir until dissolved.
3. Stir in the orange zest and juice.
4. Let the mixture cool, then blend until smooth.
5. Churn in an ice cream maker according to the manufacturer's instructions.
6. Freeze for 4-6 hours to firm up.

Elderflower and Lemon Lody

Ingredients:

- 2 cups heavy cream
- 1 cup whole milk
- 3/4 cup granulated sugar
- 2 tablespoons elderflower syrup
- Zest and juice of 1 lemon
- 1 teaspoon vanilla extract

Instructions:

1. In a saucepan, heat the heavy cream and milk over medium heat.
2. Add the sugar and stir until dissolved.
3. Stir in the elderflower syrup, lemon zest, and lemon juice.
4. Let the mixture cool, then churn in an ice cream maker.
5. Freeze for 4-6 hours until firm.

Apricot and Vanilla Lody

Ingredients:

- 2 cups heavy cream
- 1 cup whole milk
- 3/4 cup granulated sugar
- 1 cup fresh apricots (pitted and chopped)
- 1 teaspoon vanilla extract

Instructions:

1. In a saucepan, heat the heavy cream and milk over medium heat.
2. Add the sugar and stir until dissolved.
3. Cook the apricots until soft, about 10 minutes.
4. Blend the apricots into a smooth puree and mix with the cream mixture.
5. Stir in the vanilla extract and churn in an ice cream maker.
6. Freeze for 4-6 hours to firm up.

Fig and Walnut Lody

Ingredients:

- 2 cups heavy cream
- 1 cup whole milk
- 3/4 cup granulated sugar
- 1 cup dried figs (chopped)
- 1/2 cup walnuts (chopped and toasted)
- 1 teaspoon vanilla extract

Instructions:

1. In a saucepan, heat the heavy cream and milk over medium heat.
2. Add the sugar and stir until dissolved.
3. Cook the chopped figs until soft, about 10 minutes.
4. Blend the figs into a smooth puree and add to the cream mixture.
5. Stir in the vanilla extract and churn in an ice cream maker.
6. Fold in the toasted walnuts during the last few minutes of churning.
7. Freeze for 4-6 hours to firm up.

Melon and Mint Lody

Ingredients:

- 2 cups heavy cream
- 1 cup whole milk
- 3/4 cup granulated sugar
- 2 cups fresh melon (cubed)
- 1 tablespoon fresh mint (chopped)
- 1 teaspoon vanilla extract

Instructions:

1. In a saucepan, heat the heavy cream and milk over medium heat.
2. Add the sugar and stir until dissolved.
3. Puree the fresh melon and stir it into the cream mixture.
4. Add the chopped fresh mint and vanilla extract.
5. Churn in an ice cream maker.
6. Freeze for 4-6 hours to firm up.

Peach and Rosewater Lody

Ingredients:

- 2 cups heavy cream
- 1 cup whole milk
- 3/4 cup granulated sugar
- 2 ripe peaches (peeled and chopped)
- 1 tablespoon rosewater
- 1 teaspoon vanilla extract

Instructions:

1. In a saucepan, heat the heavy cream and milk over medium heat.
2. Add the sugar and stir until dissolved.
3. Cook the chopped peaches until soft, about 10 minutes.
4. Puree the peaches and stir in the rosewater and vanilla extract.
5. Churn the mixture in an ice cream maker.
6. Freeze for 4-6 hours to firm up.

Kiwi and Lime Lody

Ingredients:

- 2 cups heavy cream
- 1 cup whole milk
- 3/4 cup granulated sugar
- 2 ripe kiwis (peeled and chopped)
- Zest and juice of 2 limes
- 1 teaspoon vanilla extract

Instructions:

1. In a saucepan, heat the heavy cream and milk over medium heat.
2. Add the sugar and stir until dissolved.
3. Puree the chopped kiwis and stir in the lime zest and juice.
4. Mix the kiwi-lime puree into the cream mixture.
5. Stir in the vanilla extract and churn in an ice cream maker.
6. Freeze for 4-6 hours until firm.

Mango and Passionfruit Lody

Ingredients:

- 2 cups heavy cream
- 1 cup whole milk
- 3/4 cup granulated sugar
- 1 mango (peeled and chopped)
- 1/2 cup passionfruit pulp
- 1 teaspoon vanilla extract

Instructions:

1. In a saucepan, heat the heavy cream and milk over medium heat.
2. Add the sugar and stir until dissolved.
3. Puree the mango and mix with the passionfruit pulp.
4. Combine the fruit puree with the cream mixture.
5. Stir in the vanilla extract and churn in an ice cream maker.
6. Freeze for 4-6 hours until firm.

Coconut and Pineapple Lody

Ingredients:

- 2 cups heavy cream
- 1 cup whole milk
- 3/4 cup granulated sugar
- 1 cup pineapple chunks (fresh or canned)
- 1/2 cup shredded coconut
- 1 teaspoon vanilla extract

Instructions:

1. In a saucepan, heat the heavy cream and milk over medium heat.
2. Add the sugar and stir until dissolved.
3. Puree the pineapple chunks and stir in the shredded coconut.
4. Combine the pineapple-coconut mixture with the cream mixture.
5. Stir in the vanilla extract and churn in an ice cream maker.
6. Freeze for 4-6 hours until firm.

Banana and Peanut Butter Lody

Ingredients:

- 2 cups heavy cream
- 1 cup whole milk
- 3/4 cup granulated sugar
- 2 ripe bananas (mashed)
- 1/2 cup peanut butter
- 1 teaspoon vanilla extract

Instructions:

1. In a saucepan, heat the heavy cream and milk over medium heat.
2. Add the sugar and stir until dissolved.
3. Mash the bananas and mix with the peanut butter.
4. Stir the banana-peanut butter mixture into the cream mixture.
5. Add the vanilla extract and churn in an ice cream maker.
6. Freeze for 4-6 hours to firm up.

Peanut Butter and Chocolate Lody

Ingredients:

- 2 cups heavy cream
- 1 cup whole milk
- 3/4 cup granulated sugar
- 1/2 cup peanut butter
- 1/2 cup cocoa powder
- 1 teaspoon vanilla extract

Instructions:

1. In a saucepan, heat the heavy cream and milk over medium heat.
2. Add the sugar and stir until dissolved.
3. Whisk in the peanut butter and cocoa powder until smooth.
4. Stir in the vanilla extract and churn in an ice cream maker.
5. Freeze for 4-6 hours to firm up.

Caramel and Banana Lody

Ingredients:

- 2 cups heavy cream
- 1 cup whole milk
- 3/4 cup granulated sugar
- 2 ripe bananas (mashed)
- 1/2 cup caramel sauce
- 1 teaspoon vanilla extract

Instructions:

1. In a saucepan, heat the heavy cream and milk over medium heat.
2. Add the sugar and stir until dissolved.
3. Mash the bananas and mix with the caramel sauce.
4. Stir the banana-caramel mixture into the cream mixture.
5. Add the vanilla extract and churn in an ice cream maker.
6. Freeze for 4-6 hours to firm up.

Chocolate and Hazelnut Lody

Ingredients:

- 2 cups heavy cream
- 1 cup whole milk
- 3/4 cup granulated sugar
- 1/2 cup cocoa powder
- 1/2 cup hazelnut spread (like Nutella)
- 1 teaspoon vanilla extract
- 1/4 cup chopped hazelnuts (optional)

Instructions:

1. In a saucepan, heat the heavy cream and milk over medium heat.
2. Add the sugar and cocoa powder, stirring until dissolved.
3. Mix in the hazelnut spread until smooth.
4. Stir in the vanilla extract and churn in an ice cream maker.
5. Fold in the chopped hazelnuts during the last few minutes of churning.
6. Freeze for 4-6 hours until firm.

Chestnut and Vanilla Lody

Ingredients:

- 2 cups heavy cream
- 1 cup whole milk
- 3/4 cup granulated sugar
- 1 cup cooked chestnuts (pureed)
- 1 teaspoon vanilla extract

Instructions:

1. In a saucepan, heat the heavy cream and milk over medium heat.
2. Add the sugar and stir until dissolved.
3. Blend the cooked chestnuts into a smooth puree and stir into the cream mixture.
4. Add the vanilla extract and churn in an ice cream maker.
5. Freeze for 4-6 hours to firm up.

www.ingramcontent.com/pod-product-compliance
Lightning Source LLC
LaVergne TN
LVHW081343060526
838201LV00055B/2822